Pets in a Jar
Collecting and Caring for Small Wild Animals

Imagine having a pet that will never learn to recognize you, that will in fact ignore you, yet that is fascinating in a thousand different ways. With very little expense and a lot of imagination, you can find, catch, and keep in a glass jar many small animals such as water bugs, hydras, toads, starfish, and crickets. See for yourself how these creatures live in the environment you create for them. *Pets in a Jar* will give you your own window to nature.

BEST BOOKS OF THE YEAR, *School Library Journal*
CHILDREN'S BOOKS OF THE YEAR, Library of Congress
AN OUTSTANDING SCIENCE TRADE BOOK,
    National Science Teachers Association

pets in a jar

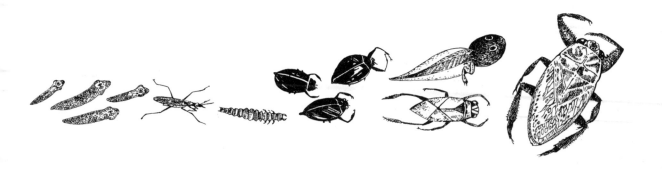

Other Puffin Science Books by Seymour Simon are

Look to the Night Sky
The Paper Airplane Book
The Secret Clocks

Seymour Simon

pets in a jar

Collecting and Caring for
Small Wild Animals

Illustrated by Betty Fraser

Puffin Books

For JOYCE
in partial repayment for the ants
in the refrigerator

PUFFIN BOOKS
Published by the Penguin Group
Penguin Books USA Inc., 375 Hudson Street, New York, New York 10014, U.S.A.
Penguin Books Ltd, 27 Wrights Lane, London W8 5TZ, England
Penguin Books Australia Ltd, Ringwood, Victoria, Australia
Penguin Books Canada Ltd, 10 Alcorn Avenue, Toronto, Ontario, Canada M4V 3B2
Penguin Books (N.Z.) Ltd, 182–190 Wairau Road, Auckland 10, New Zealand

Penguin Books Ltd, Registered Offices: Harmondsworth, Middlesex, England

First published by The Viking Press 1975
Published in Puffin Books 1979

12 13 14 15 16 17 18 19 20

Copyright © Seymour Simon, 1975
Illustrations copyright © The Viking Press, Inc., 1975
All rights reserved

Library of Congress Cataloging in Publication Data
Simon, Seymour.   Pets in a jar.
Bibliography: p.   Includes index.
Summary: Suggestions for collecting and keeping as pets such small
animals as snails, toads, worms, ants, butterflies, and starfish.
1. Vivariums—Juvenile literature. 2. Invertebrates as pets—
Juvenile literature. 3. Amphibians as pets—Juvenile literature.
[1. Vivariums. 2. Invertebrates as pets. 3. Amphibians as pets]
I. Fraser, Betty. II. Title.
SF416.2.S57 1979   639   79-1369   ISBN 0-14-049186-4

Set in Weiss Roman

Contents

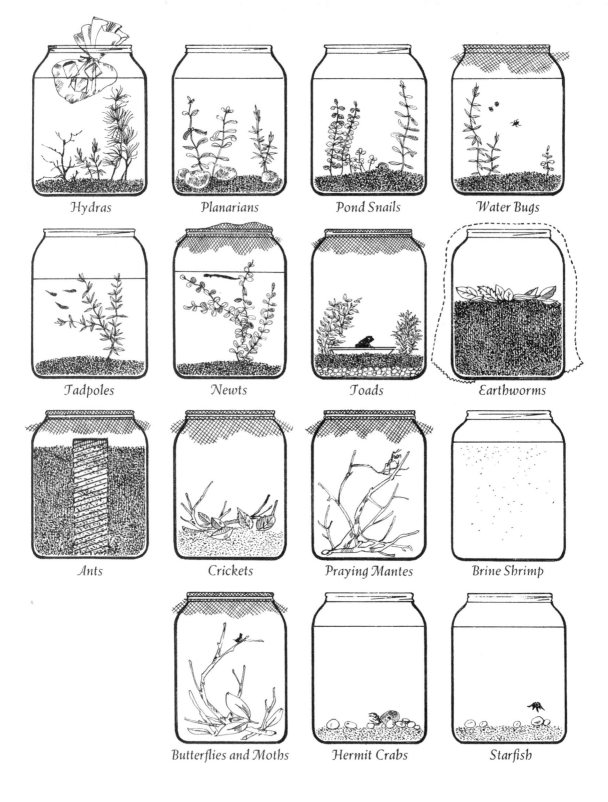

Hydras   Planarians   Pond Snails   Water Bugs

Tadpoles   Newts   Toads   Earthworms

Ants   Crickets   Praying Mantes   Brine Shrimp

Butterflies and Moths   Hermit Crabs   Starfish

Introduction: Selecting a Pet

When you hear the word pet, you usually think of a dog, a cat, a parakeet, or perhaps a hamster or gerbil. This book is about other kinds of pets: Wild animals that you can keep in a one-gallon jar in your room at home. The animals are small and easily cared for with just a little time and effort. By setting up a jar and learning to care for a wild pet, you'll find out some strange and interesting things, and enjoy yourself besides.

Dogs and cats make wonderful pets. They quickly learn to recognize you and other members of your family. They can be very affectionate, and often greet you when you come in the door. But dogs and cats are really domesticated animals. They live a life that you decide for them. Their environment is your home and they go outside when you take them out for a walk. They eat and drink what you believe is good for them. You decide whether they should be allowed to mate and have puppies or kittens. You put a collar around their necks and register them as your pets. Many dog and cat pets live more like people than like wild animals.

The wild animal pets that you meet in this book are

not at all like that. They need an environment in a container that is very similar to the environment in which they naturally live. Most, if not all, will never learn to recognize you. Most will pay no attention to you at all.

But these wild animal pets will let you see things about the way they live that are almost impossible to see in any other way. They will continue to live their natural lives as long as you supply them with an appropriate environment. You'll be able to see the way a tiny freshwater animal called a hydra uses its tentacles to catch even tinier water animals. You'll see how a quarter-inch flatworm called a planaria is able to regrow a new head, a new tail, or even two heads and two tails.

You'll be able to watch how a tadpole changes and grows and finally develops into a frog. You'll see how a caterpillar spins a chrysalis and then undergoes an enormous change to emerge as a butterfly. You'll see the hermit crab carrying its home on its back as it scurries around in a jar of seawater. No, these wild animals will never learn to recognize you. But they will interest you in a thousand different ways. A jar containing a wild pet is like a window to the world of nature.

Many of the animals you will read about in this book are easily found in a back yard, a vacant lot, a pond, or at the seashore. Some are more difficult to find, and we'll tell you where and how to look for them. Some of the other animals can be bought at a pet shop. All of the animals mentioned in this book are safe to keep.

Many wild animals are really not suited to be pets. They need special care and a great deal of attention. For this reason, you shouldn't collect just any animal you find. *Any living thing that you take home with you becomes your responsibility.* Make sure that you will be able to feed it and house it properly. Think about whether you have the time and the interest to care for it. If you don't want to care for an animal you should not collect it.

None of the animals you will read about in this book is threatened with extinction. It goes without saying that you should neither collect nor purchase any threatened species of animal. You can get up-to-date information about endangered species from zoos and museums as well as from organizations such as the National Audubon Society and the World Wildlife Fund.

Never collect more animals than you can care for properly. Leave any others where you find them. If you want to try keeping a number of different kinds of wild pets, keep a few for a short time and then release them in the same area or a similar one. Never release an animal in a place where others of its kind are not already found. Not only may it be harmed, but it may also harm the animals in the area. In many places around the world, the introduction of a foreign animal has disrupted the lives of native animals.

When you go for a walk or a collecting trip, observe the ways of the wild. Think of how the animals live in their surroundings and how they depend upon the natural world for their survival. Trying to provide similar surroundings for an animal in a jar in your home may help you to understand better what you see in the world around you.

Collecting and
Keeping Pets in a Jar

When you go out on a collecting trip to a pond, the seashore, or even to a nearby park or vacant lot, it makes sense to wear old clothing. It's also a good idea to cover your legs and arms to prevent insect bites or scratches from thorns or other plant parts. A pair of old sneakers rounds out your collecting outfit for most places. To wade into a pond, you may want a pair of high boots in addition to the sneakers.

Take along a pencil and index cards to keep notes on the observations you make. Jot down such items as the date, the time, the exact spot you catch the animal, weather conditions, temperature, other animals and plants you see nearby, and any other things you notice. The notes will come in handy when you set up a jar for the animal in your home. They'll also help you to understand how an animal survives in its environment.

Depending upon the animals that you collect, you can use many different kinds of containers to carry them home. One of the best containers is a heavy plastic bag. You can fill it with pond or ocean water and tie it closed with

a rubber band. It has the advantages of being lightweight
and at the same time of being almost unbreakable.

Glass jars are usually not a good container for collecting
in the field because they are difficult to hold on to and
break easily. Plastic containers of all kinds are much better for collecting. Another useful container for collecting trips is a plastic bucket or pail. You'll be able to see
small animals better if the pail is white or a light color
plastic.

Other useful items include a thermometer (for check-
ing air and water temperature), a small spade or shovel
(for digging and overturning rocks or logs), and a net.
The kind of net depends upon its use.

Although you can probably purchase a small fishnet
from most pet stores, you will find that it's not of much
use in catching a frog in a pond, or a butterfly on the
wing. To make a larger, more useful net at home, all you
need is an old broom or mop handle, a stiff wire clothing
hanger, adhesive or friction tape, some mesh material (see
below), and a needle and thread.

First bend the wire hanger into a loop. Twist the hook
part of the handle around the end of the broom handle
and tape it tightly in place.

The kind of mesh material you need depends upon
the use you have for the net. A water net useful for pond
or seaside animals requires a strong cloth with small holes,
such as scrim. For an insect net, use a lighter material,
such as tulle. You can use any kind of mesh material if
these are not available. Cut the material in a circle five
feet in diameter. Now fold one inch around the wire

loop. Sew this in place with a strong nylon thread. The bag should hang down about two feet to be most useful.

Practice using the net outdoors before you leave on a collecting trip. You'll find that handling the net is a bit difficult at first. Try to make short, quick sweeps with the net rather than a long, wide arc. Try to avoid catching the net in plants or bushes. If the net does get caught, try to free the mesh carefully with your hands rather than pull it away.

It's a good idea to prepare the jars you will keep the animals in at home before you collect any animals for them. The best kinds of jars to use are the one-gallon wide-mouthed glass jars used by restaurants for pickles, mustard, or ketchup. Ask the restaurant man for the empties that he throws away. If he has none on hand, explain why you want them and ask if he will save some for you.

The jars must be completely clean before you place an animal in them. Use a brush and a detergent to wash out the jar thoroughly, then rinse away all traces of the detergent under the faucet. To be sure they are clean rinse the jars several times. Even a small trace of soap or detergent can kill some sensitive water animals.

Let the jar dry completely before you set it up. In most cases, you will be using the water, soil, or plants that you collected along with the animal. If you are going to use the water from a faucet for a pond animal, you must let the water stay in an open container for at least one day. Faucet water usually contains small traces of chlorine, a substance harmful to many water animals. The chlorine will escape into the air when you let the water age.

Don't use the original screw type cover on the jar. Instead, use a nylon mesh or metal screen as a cover. This will allow air to enter the jar and at the same time keep the animal from escaping. You can use an old nylon stocking for the cover. Just cut it to the right size and fasten it in place with a rubber band.

Each animal has its own requirements for setting up the jar that is to be its home. Not every animal needs soil or saltwater. But here are some general guidelines for when you use these materials.

When you place soil in the jar, be sure not to overwater it. The jar has no drainage hole on bottom and any excess water will turn the soil soggy. This will kill some animals, such as earthworms. The water will also encourage the growth of molds and turn the soil sour. On the other hand, you must keep the soil somewhat moist. But it's better to add too little water than too much.

A jar containing a saltwater animal requires the most care of all. Mark the level of the water on the outside of the jar with a crayon when you first set it up. The water in the jar will evaporate (but not the salt). Every few days add aged fresh water up to the level that you marked. Do not let any metals come in contact with the water. Metals corrode and are poison to saltwater animals. For the same reason, make sure that no trace of soap or detergent gets into the water.

Don't use plants in a saltwater jar. The conditions of light and water chemistry are almost never just right.

Even seaweed will die and decay, spoiling the water. Fresh-water plants, of course, will not grow in seawater. To keep saltwater from turning bad, promptly remove any un-eaten bits of food from the jar.

Each animal needs a certain amount of light and a correct temperature. Generally, try to keep the animals under the same conditions in which you found them.

Many of the animals in this book can go for several days or longer without food. So don't try to feed them more than usual when you leave for a weekend trip. The excess food will probably spoil and injure the animal.

Besides observing the behavior of your pet, try to find out other things about it. Read books about the animal, using the list on page 92. Ask your teacher or librarian for some reading suggestions. Plan a trip to a nearby zoo or museum of natural history. If you can, observe the animal in its natural surroundings.

You might like to set up your own "zoo" at home or in school. Maybe your friends or classmates will help. You can use several jars to show animals in different environments. You can also experiment with some simple animals, such as brine shrimp, to see how they react to different conditions. *No experiment that you try should result in harm to an animal in your care. If you are not sure, don't try the experiment.*

It's better to begin by caring for one of the animals easier to keep, such as earthworms. Then try collecting and keeping some of the more difficult kinds. After you've read about each of the animals, you can decide which you would like to keep.

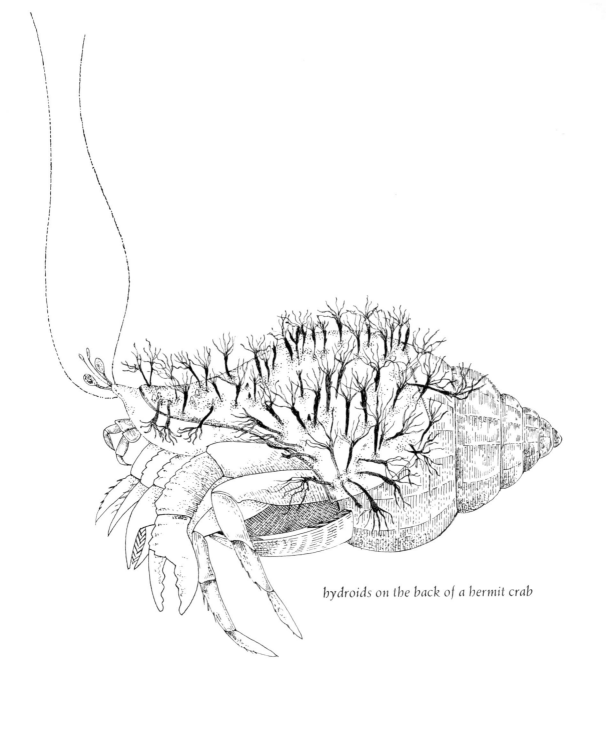

hydroids on the back of a hermit crab

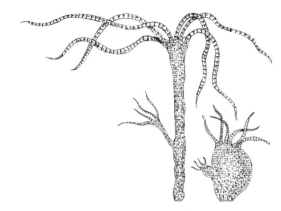

Hydras

Hydras are small freshwater animals. They attach themselves to submerged plants or other objects in ponds, lakes, and slow-moving streams. Sea-dwelling hydroids, close relatives of hydras, sometimes live in colonies on hermit crab shells. To the eye, a hydra on an underwater leaf looks like a ½-inch-long bit of thread which has become unraveled at one end. The frayed parts are really tentacles armed with poisonous stingers. Too small to hurt you, the stingers are deadly to small water animals that wander too near.

Hydras are transparent and tubelike. The tentacles, at one end of the tube, surround a slit mouth. Food is pushed through the mouth to be digested in the body region. The tentacles vary in number and size depending upon the species and the age of the hydra. At the bottom of the body is a sticky disc with which the hydra anchors itself to a leaf or a rock.

Hydras belong to a group of water-dwelling animals called *coelenterata*. The name comes from two words meaning "hollow intestines." Jellyfish, sea anemones, and corals belong to the same group. In all these animals the mouth is in the center and the body is arranged evenly around the mouth.

The hollow insides of these animals serve as the stomach. Water is circulated through the animal by the pulsing or waving of the tentacles around the mouth. Coelenterata vary in size from some so tiny that you would need a magnifying lens to see them to certain jellyfish that are six or seven feet across.

Hydras are sometimes found in large numbers in ponds or lakes when the water is cool, usually below 68° F. (20° C.). They are found in both shallow and deep water. In Lake Michigan, hydras were found covering fish nets set seventeen miles offshore in water over 100 feet deep. On the other hand, plants along the shore of a shallow pond are often coated with hydras. Of all the conditions that influence the growth and number of hydras, temperature and unpolluted water seem to be the most important.

Hydras are easy to collect. Bring several plastic bags or collecting pails to a quiet pond or lake. From along the edges of the pond, gather plants, twigs and decaying material, and some pond water. You may not be able to see any hydras in the water at first. At home, place the plants along with the water in a clean jar.

Let the water stand undisturbed for several hours. As the dirt settles and the water clears, look at the sides of the jar or the leaves of the plants. It's easier to see hydras if the jar is well lighted. If you can't find any hydras, don't be discouraged. Try collecting again at a different spot or at the same spot a few weeks later.

A dozen or more hydras should be able to live in a gallon jar for several weeks without being fed by you. In collecting hydras from a pond, you probably collected many of their food animals as well. After a while, you will have to feed the hydras. The easiest food animals to use to feed the hydras are *daphnia*, sometimes called water fleas.

Daphnia are 1/10-inch-long relatives of shrimp and lobsters. They have an oval, transparent body and two pairs of large antennae on their heads. They swim in short hops by jerking their antennae up and down. Because they move about so much, they are almost sure to bump into hydras. If you add enough daphnia to the jar, they may breed and supply the hydras with food for a long time. Almost all ponds have some daphnia; some ponds have thick clouds of the little animals. Daphnia can also be purchased in pet stores, where they are used as fish food.

Since hydras like cooler temperatures (below 70° Fahrenheit if possible), keep the jar out of the sunlight so that it will not overheat. On hot days you can keep the hydra jar cool by floating a closed plastic bag containing ice cubes in the jar.

Never add tap water to a jar containing hydras. Hydras are very sensitive to traces of copper and other materials found in tap water. Even distilled water may not be good. Always add water from the pond in which you collected the hydra. If you can't get more pond water, use water from a long-standing fish aquarium.

. You can test to see if the water is satisfactory by

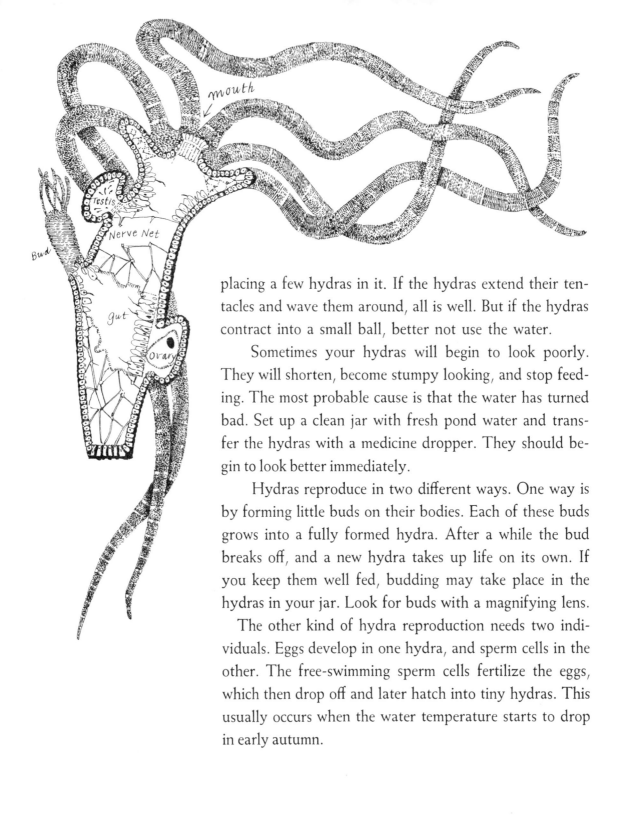

placing a few hydras in it. If the hydras extend their tentacles and wave them around, all is well. But if the hydras contract into a small ball, better not use the water.

Sometimes your hydras will begin to look poorly. They will shorten, become stumpy looking, and stop feeding. The most probable cause is that the water has turned bad. Set up a clean jar with fresh pond water and transfer the hydras with a medicine dropper. They should begin to look better immediately.

Hydras reproduce in two different ways. One way is by forming little buds on their bodies. Each of these buds grows into a fully formed hydra. After a while the bud breaks off, and a new hydra takes up life on its own. If you keep them well fed, budding may take place in the hydras in your jar. Look for buds with a magnifying lens.

The other kind of hydra reproduction needs two individuals. Eggs develop in one hydra, and sperm cells in the other. The free-swimming sperm cells fertilize the eggs, which then drop off and later hatch into tiny hydras. This usually occurs when the water temperature starts to drop in early autumn.

Hydras have the unusual ability to regrow an entire body from just a piece. This is called regeneration. You can experiment with a hydra to show regeneration. You'll need a clean medicine dropper, a one-edged razor blade, a glass microscope slide and cover slip, and a small, clean, baby food jar of pond water. *Caution: This experiment involves cutting with a sharp instrument. Do it under the supervision of a parent or teacher. Do not use a double-edged razor; it will cut your hand.*

Use the medicine dropper to nudge the hydra loose and to pick it up. Place it on the slide with a drop of water. Cover half of the body with the glass cover slip. Now use the razor to cut the body of the hydra, using the edge of the cover slip as a guide. Place each piece of the hydra in a separate baby food jar of pond water. After a few days, use a dropper to feed a daphnia to the tenacled end. In about a week, the other end should develop tentacles and can be fed.

Cutting up a hydra does not hurt it in the sense that we think of feeling pain. A hydra's nervous system is very primitive. A hydra responds to stimuli in much the same way that a plant responds to stimuli—without thinking about it. Being injured and regrowing lost parts is a natural function of hydras.

It's interesting to use a magnifying lens to view a hydra feeding on daphnia. Perhaps the best way to do this is to remove a hydra with a dropper and place it in a shallow dish with a little pond water. Then use the dropper to gently squirt a daphnia at the hydra.

In nature, hydras are active all year round, even

during winter. Many can be found beneath the ice of a pond. If you want to try collecting hydra through the ice, for your own safety be sure that you look only around the edges of the pond.

There are a number of different species of hydras. One kind, *H. littoralis,* is found only in running water. Unfortunately, this kind cannot live in a jar very well. The brown hydra, *H. oligactis,* is commonly found in still-water ponds and is a good choice for growing in a jar at home. In fact, any hydra that you find in still water can probably be kept in a jar.

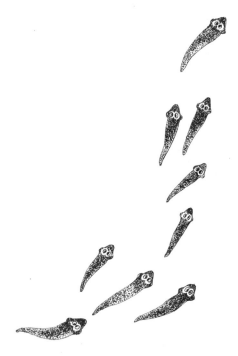

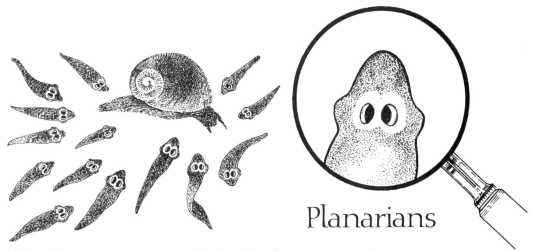

Planarians

The planarian is an unusual animal to keep as a pet in a jar. Planarians are small flatworms that live in fresh-water ponds and streams. (A few species live in salt water.) Planarians have flattened bodies, shaped something like a blade of grass, with a triangular head at one end. When mature, planarians vary from $\frac{1}{4}$-inch to 1-inch in length. You may find planarians in shades of white, gray, black, or even spotted.

Planarians glide over underwater plants and rocks searching for food. They eat small pond animals, the re-mains of dead animals that are not completely decayed, and plant cells that stick to the animal food they eat. Planarians smell their food from a distance in the water, and many may come from different directions to feed upon a dead tadpole or snail.

In fact, planaria belong to a class of animals whose name, *Turbellaria*, comes from a Latin word meaning "little crowd." When many planarians are found together, the water looks disturbed because of the motions of the tiny, hairlike cilia that cover their bodies. As the thou-sands of cilia along a planarian's body vibrate, a slimy material is discharged and forms a pathway along which the planarian glides. If you disturb a planarian, however, it will swim away rapidly, flapping its body in waves.

Looking at a planarian for the first time, you may not be able to see how it eats. It has a mouth, but it is in the middle of its body on the underside. Coming out of a planarian's mouth is a tube called the pharynx. When a planarian feeds, it hunches up, and uses its pharynx to pump up bits of the food into its mouth.

The head of a planarian has a comical, cross-eyed look. The "eye" on each side of the head has a dark spot pointing in to the center. Colorless cells cover the outward edges of the eyes. Light passes through the colorless cells, so the eyes are really sensitive to light coming from the sides. The dark spots prevent light coming from the opposite side from hitting the sensitive cells. What that means is that light coming from the left only enters the left eye, and light from the right only enters the right eye.

A planarian's eye is not very much like a human eye. It has no lens and cannot form an image the way your eye can. But it is sensitive to light and, according to one scientist, can see about as well as you do with your eyes closed. Try closing your eyes to see how you can easily tell the differences between light and dark.

In nature, planarians have few enemies. Most animals won't eat them, or will spit them out if they try. The water stages of some insects, such as dragonflies and damselflies, will sometimes eat planarians. But their worst enemies are other planarians, for they will often eat each other.

You can sometimes collect planarians by turning over small rocks and branches along the edges of a pond. Examine the undersides of the rocks carefully, for planarians usually blend in with their backgrounds. Another way to collect planarians is by using a bucket or a large, flat pan. Partly fill the bucket or pan with water. Place a handful of pond plants into the pan. Examine the leaves of the plant, the sides of the container, and the underside of the water. Planarians sometimes glide along the underside of the water's surface film.

Still another way to collect planarians is to leave bait for them. Bring along some strips of raw beef or liver on a collecting trip. Place a strip at the edge of a stream every few feet and examine the strips every half hour. Wash off any planarians you find into your collecting jar. This method works better in running water than in the quiet water of ponds. It may take a while to attract the animals, so be patient. You can try this in the winter as well as in other seasons.

At home, you can easily keep all the planarians you find in a wide-mouthed jar. Make sure the jar is clean and free of any traces of soap or detergent. Use only the water you collected from the pond, and keep an extra supply of pond water on hand in covered storage jars. Tap water is not good for planarians, but if you must use it be sure to let it age in an open container for several days. Planarians do better when the water is cool and out of direct sunlight.

Planarians can live without food for months in an extraordinary way. They use their inside organ systems as food for themselves. They will shrink in size as they use themselves up for food. If they are fed again, the planarians will regrow their organs and regain their full size.

Normally you should feed planarians two or three times a week. One way to feed them is to transfer them with a medicine dropper to another container. The feeding container should have a thin strip of raw beef or liver just barely covered with pond water. You can also try boiled egg yolk as food. Leave the planarians in the feeding jar for two or three hours. Then transfer the planarians back to their home jar. Set up the feeding jar with fresh food and water each time. This method will prevent the water in the home jar from fouling. If the water does start to smell, change the planarians into fresh pond water promptly.

Planarians may reproduce in two different ways. One method is by a planarian's splitting into two pieces, a head end and a tail end. In a few days the head end develops a new tail, and the tail end develops a new head. The other way is by laying eggs which are fertilized by another planarian. Planarians develop both male and female reproductive systems in the same individual, but the same planarian does not fertilize its own eggs.

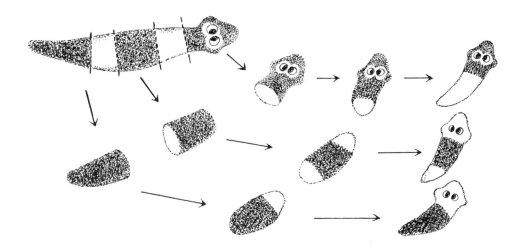

Planarians, like hydras, have a remarkable ability to regrow a whole animal from only one piece. You can experiment with this ability by using the same technique as with hydras (see page 23). Planarians will also regrow just a part of their body. If a cut is made down through the center of the head, each side will grow a new head. The

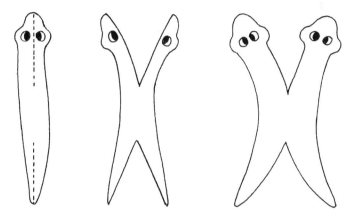

same thing is true of the tail end. So you can have a two-headed or a two-tailed planarian, or both on the same individual!

There are many different kinds of planarians. The most commonly found usually are a species of *Dugesia*. The easiest kinds to keep at home in a jar are the ones collected in the quiet water of a pond.

Many laboratory experiments are carried out on planarians. Planarians can be taught to respond in a certain way to a bright light. Even after the animal is cut up, the regenerated tail end still responds in the same way as the regenerated head end. The reasons for this and other interesting findings are still unclear.

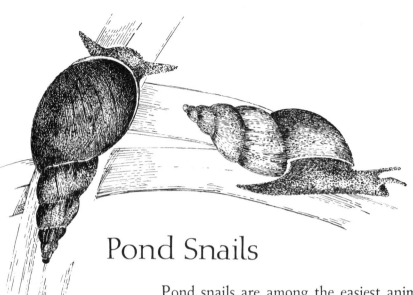

Pond Snails

Pond snails are among the easiest animals to collect and keep at home. You'll find them in freshwater ponds, lakes, and streams. You can collect snails in any clean container. Half fill the container with pond water. Lift up some of the plants growing along the edges of the pond, and place them in the container. Wait until some of the mud and other materials settle. Then look for snails clinging to the sides of the plants.

Collect some water from the pond along with a few snails and one or two water plants for your jar aquarium. Some of the water plants that will do well in a jar are Elodea, Cabomba, Spirogyra, and Nitella. At home, place the snails and plants into a clean wide-mouthed jar along with the pond water. Keep the jar where it gets some sunlight each day. If you have any pond water left, pour it into another clean jar, cover it tightly, and keep it in reserve.

Freshwater snails have two tentacles with eyes at the tips. Their shells are usually very thin and sharply pointed. Some kinds of pond snails have a little plate of hard material which they use to cover the mouth of the shell when they pull their bodies inside. This little "trap door" is called an operculum. Snails with an operculum have special gills and are able to breathe oxygen dissolved in water. They do not have to come to the surface to breathe. These snails are usually found in running water, which is rich in oxygen.

Other freshwater snails have neither an operculum nor gills. They take in some oxygen through their shells while underwater, but also have to come to the surface to get oxygen from the air. Most of these snails are found in stillwater ponds.

The common pond snail, *Physa*, is an interesting animal to watch. It crawls all over the sides of a jar and across the undersurface of the water. It breathes air as it crawls along the surface. As a pond snail travels through the water it makes thin ropes of slime. The slime ropes become paths for itself and for other snails in the jar. You can't easily see the slime paths, but the snails have no difficulty in following them.

Pond snails eat water plants or bits of dead animal material that they come across. The food is scraped off by means of a rough tongue that acts as a file. If you keep the jar in a sunny spot, it will soon develop a growth of tiny green plants called algae. Some of the algae will grow on the glass sides of the jar. When a snail crawls along the glass eating the algae, you can easily watch the action of its tongue with a magnifying lens.

A few days after you set up your snail jar, you may see little packets of stiff jelly along the sides of the jar or on the leaves of plants. The jelly packets will have little dots in them. These are snail eggs. Look at them each day with a magnifying lens. You will see the eggs develop, and after a few days they will hatch into tiny snails. Most species of snails do not have separate male and female individuals. Each snail is both. It makes both eggs and sperm. Usually the eggs of one snail are fertilized by the sperm of another snail.

As you watch a pond snail move, you will see that it sometimes gives off a string of waste matter. The string is about as thick as the lead in a pencil and may be an inch or so long. If you have a lot of snails, the bottom of the jar will soon become covered with their droppings.

If you have growing plants in the jar, the plants will use the snails' waste materials to help them grow. In the process of growing, green plants give off oxygen. In turn the snails will breathe the oxygen and eat the plants to produce more wastes. What one needs the other produces. If you have several plants and just a few snails you may have a balanced aquarium. Then the only thing you will have to add to the jar is more pond water when some evaporates.

• If the water turns green with algae you won't be able to see the snails. It's easier to prevent this than to cure it. Cut down on the amount of sunlight the jar gets each day to prevent the algae from growing so fast.

Don't add tap water directly to your snail jar. Tap water may contain chemicals which will harm the snails. Add some of the pond water you kept in reserve or let the tap water age for several days in an open container before using it. Rainwater is also good to use, if you collect it in a place where there is not much air pollution. If you live in a large city, however, you're probably better off using aged tap water.

If there are not enough plants to furnish food for the snails, add a piece of lettuce or spinach to the water every few days. Remove the uneaten remains when you add a fresh piece.

You can buy snails and plants at many pet shops if you can't collect them at a pond. Pet stores usually have pond snails as well as other kinds of snails. Try to keep other kinds such as a red Ram's Horn (Planorbis) or a Mystery Snail (Ampularia). (There really is no mystery about the Mystery Snail except, perhaps, why it's called a Mystery Snail.)

If the water in the jar starts to smell bad or turn cloudy, set up a new jar with fresh pond water right away. Transfer the snails and any plants that are still living. Discard the old water and decaying plants.

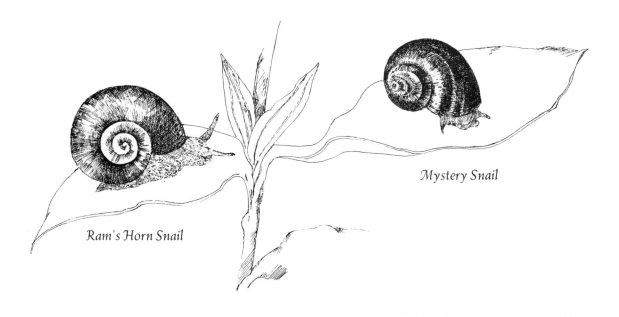

Mystery Snail

Ram's Horn Snail

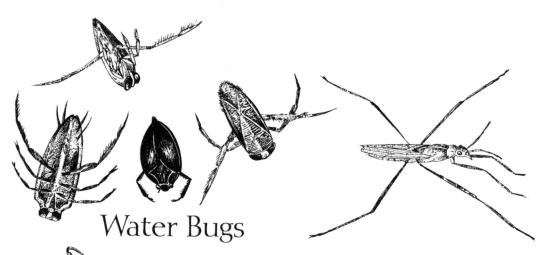

Water Bugs

Many kinds of insects such as dragonflies, damselflies, and mayflies live in the water only when they are larvae. When they become adults they leave the water to live as winged insects. But water bugs are insects that spend their entire lives in water, except when they fly from one pond to another as adults.

Water bugs include insects such as water boatmen, backswimmers, water beetles, and water scorpions. All these water bugs can be kept in a jar of pond water in your home. Although you may think they are not beautiful to look at, they do have very interesting ways of surviving in a water environment.

You can collect water bugs from most ponds during the spring, summer, or autumn. You may even find them during the winter hibernating in the mud at the bottom of a pond. Collect the insects with a bucket or a net. Also collect some pond water and a few plants for your aquarium jar.

At home set up a jar with pond water, a pond plant or two, and several of the water bugs you collected. It's a good idea to keep the top of the jar screened over to prevent any of the bugs from flying out into the room. A large water bug on the living room floor will not make you the most popular member of your family.

All water bugs are carnivorous and will eat almost any animal food small enough for them to catch. This includes tadpoles and small fishes. But their principal food is insects. You can feed water bugs with insects that you catch outside during the warmer months, such as flies, leafhoppers, and caterpillars. During the winter try feeding water bugs with mealworms. Mealworms can be purchased at most pet shops.

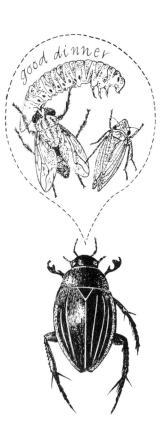

good dinner

Water boatmen swim rapidly around the aquarium jar searching for food. They use their large hind legs to kick back and propel themselves through the water. As a water boatman swims in your jar, its underside will appear a shining silver. The silver is an air bubble that the water boatman uses for breathing. The bubble is collected beneath its outer wing cover every time the boatman comes to the surface. When the air bubble is used up, the boatman darts to the top of the water, breaks through the surface film, and darts back down again.

The water beetle also traps an air bubble under its wings to breathe underwater. The water scorpion uses a long thin "snorkel" tube to breathe air from the surface. When a scorpion swims under water it has enough air left in the tube to last it for a short time.

Water bugs fly around from one pond to another, usually in hot weather when pond water contains less oxygen. The bugs often fly at night and are attracted to lights. You may find water bugs walking around on the street beneath a lamppost even in a large city. Don't try to pick one up with your bare hand. They can give a nasty bite.

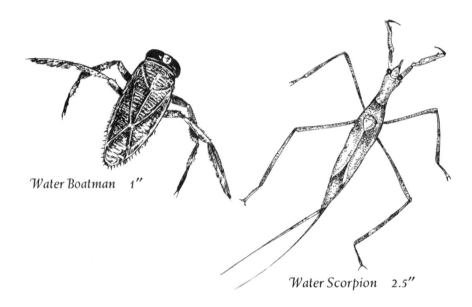

Water Boatman 1"

Water Scorpion 2.5"

The water scorpion is harder to find than the water boatman. It gets its name because its long breathing tube gives it a slight resemblance to a real scorpion. The water scorpion usually stays quietly among the plants growing along the edges of a pond. When you scoop up a bucketful of water and plants, it may contain a water scorpion, but you will have to look hard to see it. The water scorpion has a painful sting, so watch yourself. It looks like a one-inch-long brown leaf. Even if you pick a scorpion up with your fingers it won't give itself away by moving. But when you place it in your aquarium jar, it will start to walk slowly across the bottom.

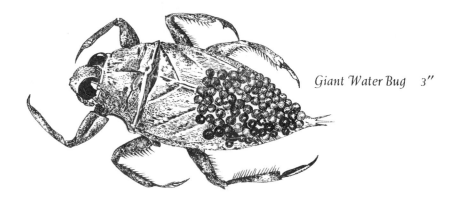

• The giant water bug, a relative of the water boat-man has an interesting way of protecting its eggs. The eggs are "glued" to the top of the male bug's back. So many eggs are stuck to the male's wing covers that it cannot fly to another pond. The giant water bug is easily able to protect itself and the eggs against most of the creatures in the pond. It has heavy front legs for grasping and a sharp beak for biting. In fact, an adult water bug can attack and kill anything from a tadpole to a small water snake.

Water striders, strictly speaking, are not water bugs, but they are interesting insects to keep in an aquarium jar. Water striders are able to walk on the surface of the

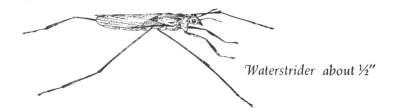

Waterstrider about ½"

water by keeping their feet dry. The hind legs have fine hairs which skate rapidly along the water film. These legs must be lifted up often to keep the hairs dry, or the insect may sink and drown. When you put your hand in the water near a water strider, it just skates quickly away in response to water vibrations. Water striders feed on the juices of both living and dead insects which fall on the water of a pond. You'll have to supply a strider with insects if you want to keep it as a pet in a jar.

Keep a water bug jar in a cool place in your house. Cool water can hold more oxygen than warm water. For the same reason, keep the jar out of direct sunlight. Do you see any difference in behavior at different water temperatures?

Each pair of legs on a water boatman serves a special purpose. The front, short legs are used to hunt through the material on the bottom for food. The middle legs are used for holding on to a plant stem or a stone when the water boatman is resting. A boatman's long, oar-like hind legs are used to push it through the water. Observe if this is always the way the legs are used.

How long can a water bug stay under water without resupplying its air bubble? That depends upon the water temperature and how active the bug is. But at least one kind of water bug has been known to stay underwater for more than a day and a half, without changing its air supply. For how long does a water bug stay submerged in your jar?

To show how back swimmers and water bugs respond to vibrations in the water, place a bit of raw meat on the surface of the water. Since the meat is not moving the way an insect would, it will probably be ignored. Now stick the same piece of meat at the end of a toothpick and wiggle it at the surface. It should be attacked immediately. By the way, don't wiggle your fingers in the water or you might receive a painful bite.

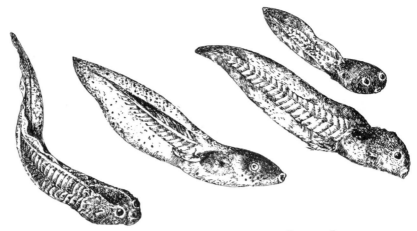

Tadpoles

Frogs live on all the continents of the world, although most frogs are found in the Northern Hemisphere. About twenty different kinds of frogs are found in the United States. Frogs can live almost anywhere if there is enough freshwater. Frogs can even be found in springs in the desert. About March or April, you can often find frogs' eggs in ditches temporarily flooded by rainwater.

The exception to this are bullfrog tadpoles. These need permanent ponds or lakes because they may take as long as three years to change into their adult form. Bullfrog tadpoles can be surprisingly large. In their third year just before the tail is absorbed, they may be six to eight inches in length. But by the time a bullfrog is ready to leave the water minus its tail, it will only measure about two inches. The larger tadpoles won't do as well as the smaller ones when you keep them in a jar.

If you go to a pond in the springtime, you'll probably be able to collect frogs' eggs as well as tadpoles. Take along a long-handled net (see page 14) and a few strong plastic bags or a covered plastic container. You may be

able to capture adult frogs with your net, but these need larger quarters than a gallon jar can provide, and should be released.

Frogs' eggs look like small black beads surrounded by jelly. You'll find them in clumps of hundreds or even thousands. Scoop up about a dozen eggs and place them in a jar or plastic bag along with some pond water. Look for tadpoles clinging to plants along the edges of the pond. Sweep the net through the water to catch a few of the tadpoles. Place them in the container along with pond water and some pond plants.

Some of the common species of frogs that you may find around a pond in the spring are the Meadow or Leopard frog (*Rana pipiens*), the Pickerel frog (*R. palustis*), the Green frog (*R. clamitans*), and the Bullfrog (*R. catesbeiana*).

At home, set up two separate jars, one for the eggs and the other for the tadpoles. Each jar should be kept about three quarters full of pond water. Keep plants in the tadpole jar but not in the jar with the eggs. Keep the jars at room temperature, away from the sun or a radiator.

In a warm room frogs' eggs will develop and hatch in about a week. Cooler temperatures will delay their hatching. Use a magnifying lens to examine an egg. Each egg has a black part and a white part. The white part is the yolk. It is used for food by the developing tadpole. Each day you can see changes in the dark part. You'll see the head and the tail of a tadpole develop. You'll see the tadpole begin to move in the jelly.

One day the egg will hatch and a tiny tadpole will

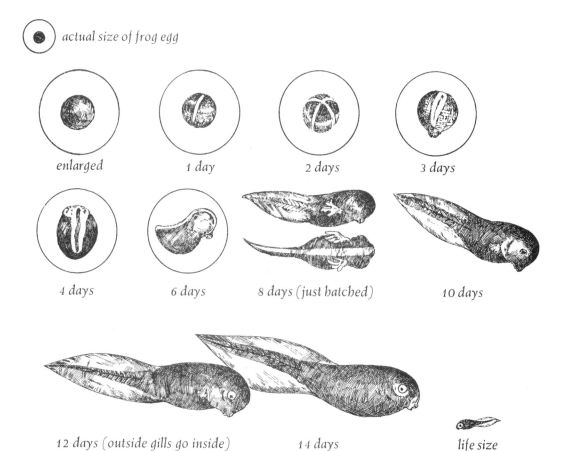

actual size of frog egg

enlarged   1 day   2 days   3 days

4 days   6 days   8 days (just hatched)   10 days

12 days (outside gills go inside)   14 days   life size

wiggle away. Place a pond plant into the jar. The tadpole will soon attach itself with two sticky cups atop its head to a leaf of the plant. A tadpole has no mouth at first. Look for the gills behind its head. A newly hatched tadpole breathes through its gills and feeds from the attached yolk.

In a few days, the tadpoles will grow larger and begin to swim around in the jar. Their mouths open and they begin to feed. You should supply the tadpoles with plant

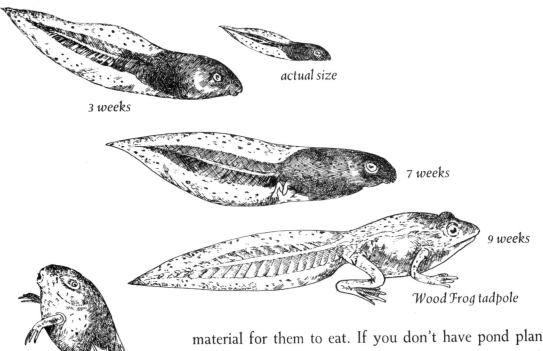

3 weeks

actual size

7 weeks

9 weeks

Wood Frog tadpole

Bullfrog Tadpoles

material for them to eat. If you don't have pond plants, add a bit of boiled spinach or lettuce. You can keep five or six tadpoles in a one-gallon jar. Return the extra tadpoles to a pond or set up another jar for them.

In a few months (with bullfrog tadpoles it takes two years), your tadpoles will start to develop legs. The tads are beginning to turn into frogs. As soon as their hind legs develop completely, their front legs appear. Their bodies grow compact and change shape.

Inside each tadpole great changes are taking place. Lungs develop, and the tadpole begins to breathe at the surface of the water. After a while the tail disappears and you have a tiny frog. Place a float made of wood or light plastic in the jar so that the newly formed frog can rest.

The development of a frog from the first signs of legs to the disappearance of the tail takes about a month. This gives you time to decide what to do with your frog. If you are going to keep adult frogs you will need a larger container, such as a ten-gallon aquarium tank.

Frogs eat insects and other animal foods. A frog's food has to be moving and must be small enough to be swallowed whole. Frogs need a place to sit as well as water to swim in. A large rock in their aquarium provides a good resting place. Be sure to cover a frog aquarium with a metal or plastic screen to prevent them from jumping out. If you cannot provide these things for your frogs, return them to a pond.

•   Water temperature is important in determining the time it takes for eggs to hatch and tadpoles to develop. You might want to experiment by keeping some eggs in a jar outside your home where it is colder. Compare their development to the eggs in a jar kept in a warm room.

Don't keep large tadpoles and small tadpoles in the same jar. Some kinds of large tadpoles eat smaller ones. Large fish, snakes, turtles, and the water stages of certain insects such as the dragonfly nymph and the water beetle, are fond of a tadpole meal. In nature, only a few tadpoles survive to become adult frogs.

When you collect tadpoles and eggs from a pond, don't leave the container in direct sunlight for more than a few minutes. The water in it will heat up and the tadpoles may die. For the same reason, don't leave the container right beneath a car heater, or atop a radiator when you get home.

Newts

In the spring, if you go to a pond to collect tadpoles, you may also find newts breeding in the cold water. You'll see them floating just beneath the surface. Newts are salamanders. Salamanders, along with frogs and toads, belong to a class of animals called amphibians—animals that live both on land and in water. Amphibians spend the first part of their lives breathing through gills underwater and the second part breathing through lungs. Amphibians have a smooth moist skin and will die if they dry out. All amphibians must lay their eggs either in water or in a moist place.

The common Eastern or red-spotted newt (*Diemictylus viridescens*) is found from Florida to Canada and as far west as Texas. The Western or Pacific newt (*Taricha torosus*) is sometimes called the water dog. Both kinds are easily kept and fed in a jar at home.

Catch newts with a net or, if you don't mind getting wet, with your hands. Hold the newts firmly and drop them into a container. Collect only two or three per one-gallon jar. Also collect some pond water and a few pond plants.

At home, set up a clean jar with some pond water and a few plants. The newts will often rest on the plants. Cover the jar tightly with a screen or a piece of nylon stocking held in place with a rubber band. Newts can easily climb out of an uncovered jar and may end up dried and lifeless beneath a piece of furniture.

A newt will eat almost any small pond animal. In nature, a newt eats daphnia, water insects, tadpoles, frogs' eggs, worms, and small fishes. If you can feed any of these to your newts, they will do just fine. But if these foods are not easily available, try feeding small bits of lean meat or canned dog food. Another good food for newts is Tubifex, small red worms sold in tropical fish shops.

An adult red-spotted newt is about three or four inches long. The newt's color is greenish or yellow, and it has a row of black-circled red dots along its sides. Its tail is flattened and used for swimming. Just before the spring breeding season, a male's tail becomes wavy. A female newt's body is plumper and has thinner back legs.

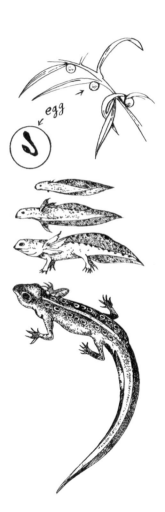

egg

A female newt lays about one hundred eggs. These are fertilized underwater by the male's sperm. The eggs stick to parts of underwater plants. Depending upon water temperature, newt eggs hatch in twenty to thirty days. Newt larvae are about one quarter of an inch long. They have gills to breathe underwater. In a few days legs sprout, first front ones and then hind ones.

After a few months as a larva, a newt begins to change. It is entering its land-dwelling stage. It is about one inch long now. Its color is an orange red, but it still has black-circled dots along its sides. The best place to find it in this

stage is in a forest after a rain, as it crawls about under the wet leaves or a clump of moss. At this stage, a newt is called a red eft. Its skin is rougher than before and a little grainy. If you put it under water, a thin, silvery film of air coats its body beneath the surface. If you collect an eft from a forest, you are better off keeping it in a jar with some mosses and ferns. Be sure to keep the jar moist and covered. Feed an eft small earthworms or cut up bits of larger ones. Efts are more picky when it comes to eating than adult newts, and may not take any food unless it is moving. In nature, an eft eats small insects such as mosquitoes, flies, spiders, worms, and small snails. During dry weather, an eft remains hidden in a moist log or a crack in the ground. But after a rain or when it's foggy, an eft hunts for food both day and night.

An eft must return to water to become an adult. After a year or so on land, efts head toward a pond or stream in groups. Here efts change into the form that you see swimming in the water. They remain water newts for the rest of their lives, perhaps two or three years.

The Western newt found along the west coast of the United States goes through much the same changes as its eastern relative. But a western newt may leave the water and go back to the land even after it has become an adult. This helps the newt survive in places where ponds and streams dry up quickly during a dry spell.

• In some places, such as Long Island in New York State, living conditions such as moist forest lands are not available to the land stage of the newt. In these areas newt larvae change directly into adults without becoming efts.

Try to collect newt eggs in the spring. Each egg is surrounded by a round glob of jelly that forms a mass around the stem or leaves of a pond plant. Keep about a dozen newt eggs in a jar with some pond water. Observe how the eggs develop each day. When the larvae hatch, they breathe through feathery external gills. Newly hatched larvae will eat any smaller animals that move through the water. Try feeding larvae with daphnia (see page 21). If you can't obtain food for the larvae, return them to the pond.

If the water in the jar begins to smell bad, replace it with some fresh pond water or some tap water that has aged for a few days.

If you can't find earthworms for a red eft, and it won't eat the motionless food you leave in its jar, place a bit of chopped meat on a thread and dangle it in front of the eft. Keep the meat moving until the eft goes for it. Be patient; it may take a while.

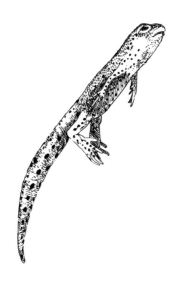

Fowler's Toad

Toads

The rough, warty skin of a toad helps you to tell it apart from a frog. A toad's skin absorbs water very easily when it is submerged but doesn't give off water in dry surroundings. A toad's skin, along with more efficient lungs than those of a frog, allows the toad to spend much of its time out of the water.

Toads don't leap as frogs do but move along in short hops. Sometimes, when going after an insect, toads break into a kind of fast shuffle that gets them close to their prey without alarming it. A toad doesn't have to get right on top of an insect to grab it. A few inches away, the toad stops and turns its head from side to side. Suddenly, a sticky tongue flicks out, captures the insect and throws it into the back of the toad's mouth. The long tongue is attached to the front of a toad's mouth and moves almost too fast to be seen.

In the spring you may find hundreds of tiny toads, no more than one half of an inch long, around ponds. They have just developed from a tadpole stage. In a few weeks, however, the toadlets begin to travel away from the water of the pond to spend their adult lives on dry land. They usually move during damp or rainy weather.

Toads are very helpful animals to a farmer. Some scientists estimate that a toad will eat several hundred harmful insects each night during the summer. Toads do not upset the balance of nature by killing other animals as do some poisonous insecticides.

You can find toads in almost every section of the United States. In the eastern states, the American toad (*Bufo americanus*) is common in gardens and backyards. It spends the day in a damp, sheltered spot. At night it comes out to hunt for insects and earthworms. Use a flashlight to look for it hopping over the ground.

In the Southeast, the oak toad (*B. quercicus*) is a small toad that makes a tremendous piping noise when it congregates in thousands around ponds and ditches. Other toads that you may find in the eastern and central parts of the United States are the common toad (*B. terrestris*) and Fowler's toad (*B. woodhousei fowleri*). The western states have larger toads, but they are not suitable for keeping in a jar.

In northern regions, toads hibernate as soon as cooler weather sets in. They burrow backwards into loose soil. Often toads will dig and shovel until they are several feet beneath the surface of the ground. Toads will spend the winter huddled together in a small chamber below the ground. In the spring when the outside air temperature reaches about 50° they will come out.

You can keep one toad of average size in a one-gallon jar. Set up the jar as a terrarium. First put down a one-

saucer with water

soil

pebbles or gravel

inch layer of small pebbles or coarse gravel. This will provide drainage. Spread soil on top of the gravel. Place some mosses or a few small woodland plants on the surface of the soil. Sink a deep saucer into the soil. Keep it filled with water. The toad will soak in the water from time to time.

Cover the top of the jar with a screen to prevent the toad from climbing out. Keep the jar at room temperature but not in direct sunlight. The soil in the jar should be kept moist by sprinkling it with water every other day.

The best time to catch toads is at night. Use a flashlight to look for them. You'll find toads active during the warmer months of the year. Look in back yards or gardens, in grassy fields of a nearby park, or around ponds or ditches in the spring. Use your hands or a net to capture a toad when you see it. Bring along a collecting jar which contains some damp moss or wet leaves, making sure the cover of the jar has air holes.

No matter what your friends say, you can't get warts from handling a toad. The warts on a toad protect it from being grabbed by a larger animal such as a dog. The warts contain glands which give off a white fluid. The fluid is very irritating to the mouth parts of a large animal. Unfortunately for the toad, the fluid doesn't prevent it from being eaten by some snakes. The fluid won't bother you as long as you don't get it into your eyes or mouth. *That's why it's a good idea to wash up after touching a toad.*

At home, place the toad in your terrarium jar. Cover the jar promptly. Don't attempt to feed the toad as soon as you place it in the jar. Toads can go for several days without eating.

You can feed your toad two or three times a week. Toads are eager eaters of earthworms and caterpillars. They'll also eat such insects as crickets and grasshoppers.

During the colder months when insects are difficult to find, try feeding your pet toad with a bit of canned dog food or scraped lean beef. Stick the meat at the end of a thread and move it back and forth in front of the toad. Toads will only go after a moving object. So keep trying and be patient. A toad will usually learn to eat meat from a moving thread.

If the jar develops a bad odor, remove the toad and clean the jar with soap and water. Set up the jar as before. You may have to clean the jar every other month.

There are many legends about toads. One is that a toad once wore a jewel in its head called a toadstone. The jewel was stolen and in its place the toad has only the gold and black sparkle of its eyes. Other legends relate that toads can live for hundreds of years holed up in an enclosed space, without food or water. These legends are enjoyable to read about, but not very factual. The truth is that the toad is an interesting animal to keep and observe, but not magical or mysterious in any way.

Toads learn some things very quickly. For example, a toad placed on a table will soon learn to hesitate at the edge before it jumps. Frogs, on the other hand, keep jumping off a table no matter how many times they try. Toads also will quickly learn to reject an unpleasant food, while frogs take a much longer time to learn.

See if you can teach a toad to accept food from your hand. Does the toad ever learn to come over when you place your hand in the jar? What other kinds of behavior may tend to show that a toad has learned something?

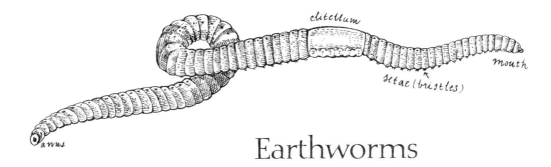

clitellum

mouth

setae (bristles)

anus

Earthworms

The great scientist Charles Darwin was the first to write about the importance of earthworms to the soil. He estimated that one acre of land contained about fifty thousand earthworms. During the space of a single year, the worms overturn more than fifteen tons of soil. Over a twenty-year span, several inches of a new layer of soil will cover the ground.

Earthworms live in all parts of the world where the soil is suitable, that is, damp but not swampy. You can see that earthworms leave their burrows in great numbers after a heavy rainfall. Their bodies sometimes cover the ground. This gave rise to an old superstition that worms "rain down" during a downpour. It would be more accurate to say that the worms are "rained up" from their burrows.

There are many different kinds of earthworms. Some are found only in certain kinds of soil. Others are found in many different kinds of soil. In the United States, a common earthworm is rarely larger than eight or nine inches in length. But in Australia one kind of earthworm grows to over ten feet in length.

Earthworms are easy animals to collect and keep at home. They are active at night, when they emerge on the surface of the soil to gather leaves and drag them underground to feed upon. You can collect earthworms by flashlight, or you can collect them during daylight hours by digging for them. Look for worms in any spot where the soil contains rotting plant materials.

Collect about half a dozen worms along with enough soil to half fill a wide-mouthed jar. Also collect some of the leaves you find on the ground.

At home, place a layer of leaves atop the soil in the jar. Place the jar in the coolest spot in your home (but *not* in the refrigerator). Be sure to keep the jar out of direct sunlight and away from a radiator. Wrap some dark paper around the jar to keep out light. Remove the paper when you want to observe the worms.

Every few days, sprinkle a few drops of water on the soil. Keep the soil moist but not soggy. Too much water will turn the soil bad and kill the worms. Use celery leaves, lettuce, and other cut-up vegetable scraps as food for the worms. Keep track of which they seem to eat. Don't overfeed them and be sure to remove any food that starts to spoil.

Observe how the worms tunnel through the soil in the jar. Do they seem to be eating? How do they move their bodies? Watch the mouth of a worm as it moves against the glass. What happens when a worm comes to the surface of the soil? Watch how it drags a leaf down into the soil.

Earthworms burrow through the soil both by eating it

and by pushing it aside. The worms leave castings of digested leaves and other matter which help enrich the soil. They also improve the soil because their tunnels make it easier for air and water to enter. As worms burrow up and down in the soil, they turn over the layers. This mixes them up and improves them for farming. Earthworms cannot make poor soil into good soil. But they do help to keep soil in good condition for planting crops. It's no wonder that they are called "the farmer's friend."

Take out a worm and examine it with your eyes and with your fingers. The tiny bristles on the underside of a worm are called setae. They help the worm dig into the soil when it moves its body.

Place the worm on a damp paper towel and watch how it moves. One part of the worm stretches out while another part squeezes together. The bunched up part grips the paper with its setae, while the end part is pulled forward. Then another part squeezes together and so on.

An earthworm can move like this because of the way its body is made. A worm's body has rings of hard material joined together with bands of softer material. Each of the bands is called a segment. Try to count the segments on a worm. Older worms may have from 100 to over 200 segments. Younger worms have fewer segments.

It may not be easy to decide which end of the worm is the front end. Of course, the mouth is at the front, but it may not be easy to spot. Here's how to tell. See if the worm has a wide, light-colored saddle on its body. This is called a *clitellum*, and it is located about one third toward the front end of the worm.

Each earthworm produces both sperm and egg cells for reproduction. But an earthworm must interchange sperm with another earthworm to fertilize its own eggs. After the eggs are fertilized, the clitellum makes a jelly-like ring around the worm. The ring moves down over the body, picks up the fertilized eggs, and is deposited in the soil. The ring thus becomes a protective cocoon in which the young worms hatch.

Earthworm cocoons are yellowish in color and about as large as a pinhead. Can you see any cocoons in the soil of the jar? They may be hard to spot, but if you can maintain worms in a jar long enough, the eggs may hatch and you will see small worms in the soil.

There are a number of different species of earthworms all over the world. The one that you will probably collect is the common earthworm, *Lumbricus terrestris*. If you were to collect worms in a cow pasture, another common worm you might find is the fecal earthworm, *Eisenia foetida*. Either kind can easily be kept in a jar at home.

You might have some trouble in keeping one kind of Australian earthworm. These average four feet in length, and some individual worms are reported to be over ten feet long! Can you imagine going fishing with one of these monster-sized earthworms?

• Even though earthworms have no eyes, they are sensitive to light at different spots along their bodies. You can easily experiment with their sensitivity to light. Punch a small hole in the center of a cardboard disc. Tape the disc over a flashlight. In a darkened room, shine a spot of light on different parts of an earthworm's body. Note how it responds to the light by moving. Can you tell whether the head region is more sensitive to light than the middle of the worm? Is the tail region sensitive to light?

Earthworms are sensitive to vibrations. That's why they retreat into their tunnels when they feel an approaching footstep. You can show how the earthworms in your jar respond to vibrations by tapping the table upon which their jar is resting. What do the worms do? See if they will respond to a very light tap or only to a heavy one.

Earthworms are often used in laboratories as subjects in various kinds of research. They can regenerate a tail if they do not lose too much of it. (But they are not nearly as good a subject for regeneration experiments as hydras or planarians.) Earthworms are also used in learning experiments, where they have been shown to learn certain kinds of responses. To find out more about these experiments, and how you might go about trying some, read some of the books listed on page 92.

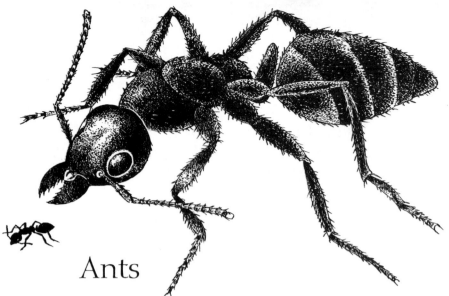

Ants

There are many kinds of ants. They are found in different sizes and several colors. But all ants live in groups with other ants of the same species. Because of the way they live with others of their kind, ants are called social insects. Bees and termites are two other examples of social insects.

To survive for any length of time, an ant colony must have a queen. The queen is not the ruler of an ant colony in the way a human queen may be the ruler of a country. Rather, a queen ant lays the eggs from which all the other ants develop. In most cases, the queen has also founded the colony.

At one time, the queen was a young winged ant in another colony. At that time of the year there are many other winged ants in the colony. Some, the larger winged ones, are females. The smaller winged ones are males.

For some still unknown reason, there comes a day when all the winged ants are pushed and carried outside by the other ants. For the first time they try out their wings. They leave the ground in thick swarms. At the same time, the same thing is happening in nearby colonies of that species.

With most species of ants, the act of mating is done on the wing. As soon as they mate, the winged ants land. The more numerous males soon die or are eaten by birds or other animals. The females seek a place in which to hide. They tear off their wings and look for a place to start a new colony.

At first, the new queen lays just a few eggs. She tends these for weeks while they pass through the stages of development. When they become adults these ants are known as workers. The first workers are small compared to workers that are born later. But these small workers take on all the chores of the nest. They go out and find food and bring it back to share with the rest of the colony. They care for the new eggs and the young that develop. They build tunnels, keep the nest clean, and defend it if necessary. As other workers become adults, the colony grows. Some kinds of ants have a special kind of worker called a soldier. The soldier has a large head and powerful jaws, and its job is defense.

Some species of ants tunnel through soil to build nests. It is interesting to watch ants at work building the tunnels. Here's how to set up a jar so that you can see how the ants work together to make a nest. Put a block of wood in the middle of a jar. Then pack soil around the block. This will force the ants to tunnel around the wood close to the glass sides of the jar where you can see them more easily. You'll also need a cover made of fine mesh screening or an old nylon stocking. Be sure the cover is fastened tightly with rubber bands or tape to prevent the ants from invading your house.

You'll need some plastic bags, rubber bands, some newspapers, a shovel, and a large spoon to help you collect ants. Look for ants under rocks or rotting logs. You may spot the telltale anthill that some kinds make. A common species of ant that you may find in a nearby field or vacant lot is a small to medium-sized black ant.

When you find the entrance to an ant nest, spread out a newspaper on the ground nearby. Dig down into the soil with your shovel and place the loose soil on the newspaper. Try to spot ants, small white ant eggs, larger ant cocoons, and small wriggling larvae. Use the spoon to place these in a plastic bag.

queen ant rubbing off her wings

Look carefully for an ant that is much larger than any of the others. This is a queen. Without a queen, ants will dig tunnels and live for a while in a jar. But the colony will soon die. Sometimes a queen will crawl under the paper to hide. Be sure to lift up the newspaper and look.

At home, place the plastic bag containing the ants in the refrigerator (not the freezer) for about one hour. This will slow down the ants so that you can more easily transfer them into the jar. The actual transfer is best done outside, so that any ants that escape will not become unwelcome house guests. Place the contents of the chilled bag on some newspaper spread out on the ground. Working quickly, transfer the ants, along with eggs, cocoons, and larvae, into the jar. Then cover the jar and bring it inside.

It's a good idea to wrap some dark paper around the

sides of the jar. Hold the paper in place with a rubber band. This will encourage the ants to build tunnels next to the glass where it is dark. Remove the paper when you want to observe the ants. Leave the jar undisturbed for a few days, so that the ants can get used to their new surroundings.

Ants will do best at ordinary room temperatures, not in direct sunlight or near a radiator. Keep the soil moist but not soggy by adding a few drops of water when needed. Don't add too much water or mold will grow.

After the first few days, place the ants on a regular feeding routine. Try feeding your ants with a few bits of a vegetable or a fruit, some crumbs of bread or cereal, a scrap of meat, or a few drops of sugar water. Use a small piece of cardboard as a feeding dish. Place the cardboard on the surface of the soil.

Every other day remove the cardboard and replace the food on it with fresh food. Note which foods the ants seem to eat. Try to vary the diet with scraps you have left over from your own meals. Don't feed the ants too much and be sure to replace food before it spoils.

When you observe the ants, keeping the paper off for a long time is better than moving it off and on every few minutes. You should be able to see ants building tunnels the first time you look.

• A magnifying lens will help you to observe the ants more closely. Look carefully at an individual ant. Notice its large eyes and strong jaws. The head is attached to the thorax (chest) by a short neck. The thorax and abdomen (stomach) are connected by a thin waist. Ants,

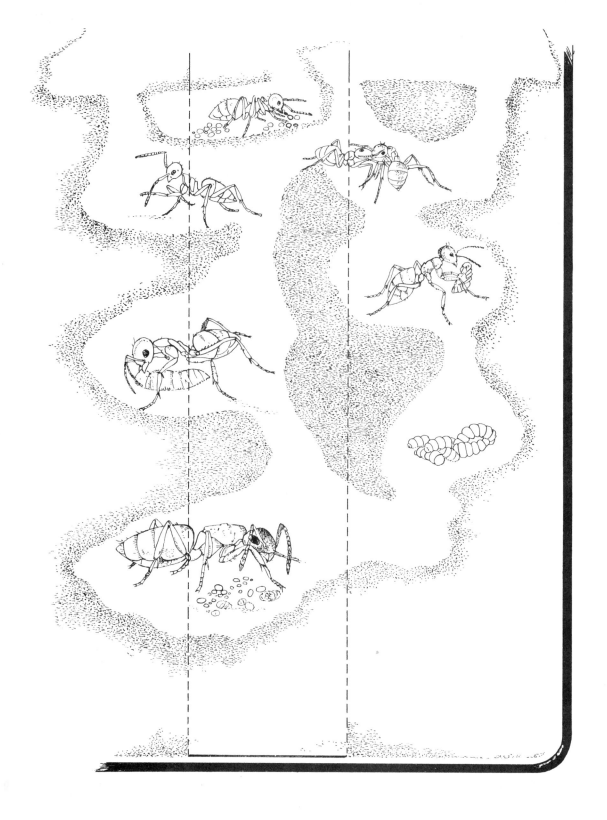

like all other insects, have six legs. Do you see how an ant's legs are adapted to stick onto surfaces?

Ants depend on odor to recognize one another, to tell which food to eat, and to find their way. Observe what happens when an ant meets another ant, and the way in which an ant seems to recognize another ant from its own nest.

What do you think would happen if you introduced a different kind of ant into the jar, or if you removed an ant from the jar and replaced it after a few days? Does the odor of the nest seem to wear off?

Does temperature or the amount of light on the jar influence tunnel building, and does it have an effect on other ant activities? How can you experiment to find out?

If you have a queen in your jar it will lay eggs. The eggs hatch into wriggling larvae, which then form a cocoon. Eventually they become worker ants. If you have a queen, see if you can observe all these stages in an ant's development within your jar. How is each stage cared for by the worker ants? Does the queen have anything to do with caring for the eggs or larvae? Read about what scientists say (see page 92) to see if your observations are confirmed.

You can provide your ants with trails to go out and find food. Use plastic tubing (you can buy this in a pet store that sells tropical fish) to make trails to other jars. Set these up with food, being sure to secure the tubing with tape and rubber bands so that the ants can't escape.

Crickets

Crickets are easily kept and cared for, interesting to watch, and are very musical besides. A cricket in a jar will start to chirp, usually in the early evening, and keep up a pleasant chorus for hours.

There are several different kinds of crickets in the United States, but you'll most often find the common black field cricket, *Gryllus assimilis*. Field crickets live under rocks, boards, decaying logs, in the grass, or almost anywhere on the ground. Watch carefully when a cricket jumps to see where it lands. Then try catching it with your cupped hand or with a net or paper bag. Carefully transfer the captured cricket to a container.

At home, place some sand at the bottom of a jar along with a few twigs and some leaves. Keep the sand moist but not soggy. Place the cricket in the jar. Be sure you keep the jar covered with screening.

Crickets do best in shady places out of direct sunlight. They will eat almost any kind of food. Try giving them bits of cut up potatoes, apples, or some other fruit or vegetable. Crickets will also eat bits of meat. If you feed your crickets with some juicy foods such as a bit of fruit each day, they will not need any extra water. Otherwise place a piece of moist cotton in the jar. If you don't want to keep watering the cotton every day, you can use a test tube filled with water and plugged with cotton as a water supply. Just lay the test tube flat on the bottom of the jar.

Check the food in the jar each day to see that it has not spoiled. Remove any spoiled food and replace it with fresh food. Make sure the cricket has enough water. The cricket's song will tell you that all is well.

It's not a good idea to keep more than one male cricket in a one-gallon jar. Male crickets fight among themselves, and the loser may pay with its life. You can tell a male cricket from a female cricket by comparing the back ends of their bodies. A female cricket has a long tube projecting from the back. The tube, called an ovipositer, is used to lay eggs in the ground. The male cricket has no such tube.

Crickets do not show the great physical change from stage to stage that other insects, such as butterflies, do. Cricket eggs are deposited in the soil sometime in the fall and remain there throughout the winter. With the arrival of warmer weather in the spring, the eggs hatch into small crickets called nymphs. The nymphs look much like the adult crickets. The young nymphs feed and grow. When they become too big for their outer skin, the skin splits and a new larger skin forms and hardens. This is called molting. Crickets molt a number of times before they become adults.

Only a male cricket chirps. The chirp is produced when one wing is drawn across the other. The hard, rough surface on the underside of the wing is pulled across a hardened vein on the upper front of the other wing. The wing vibrates and makes the sound. Some crickets chirp right wing over left wing and others chirp left wing over right. (Check your cricket to see whether it is a "righty" or a "lefty." Most crickets chirp right wing over left wing.)

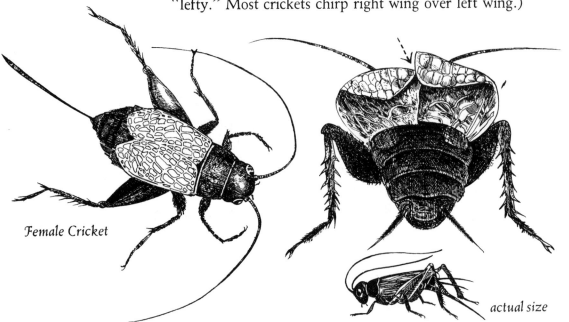

Female Cricket

actual size

The cricket's song is not just for your enjoyment. One kind of chirp is used to attract a female. Another chirp is used as a warning to other males. Although people cannot easily tell the songs apart, crickets seem to have no difficulty. Scientists have recorded cricket songs in an effort to tell one kind of song from another.

Crickets are highly prized for their songs in China and

Japan. The cricket is kept in a small bamboo cage so it can be fed and its song heard. Still another way crickets are enjoyed in the Orient is as fighters. Wagers are placed on the fights and good fighting crickets are highly prized.

• Crickets' songs speed up in warm weather and slow down in cooler weather. In fact, it may be possible to estimate the temperature by counting the number of chirps in one minute and using this formula worked out by a scientist.

$$\text{Temperature} = 50 + \frac{N - 40}{4}$$

N stands for the number of chirps in one minute. This usually is not very accurate. One reason is that the field cricket is not as reliable a chirper as the snowy tree crickets upon which the formula was based. Another reason is that it is awfully hard to tell when one chirp ends and another begins.

If you have a male and a female cricket in your jar, and they mate, the female will lay eggs in the soil. Keep the soil in the jar moist over the winter. If the eggs hatch and nymphs appear in the jar in the spring, feed them the same foods that the adults eat.

While field crickets in a jar make good pets, house crickets on the loose are not desirable. These small, pale relatives of the field cricket are likely to be found in warm spots near a furnace or radiator. They will eat anything, from crumbs to carpets and even clothing. If you can overlook the damage they do, they will repay your hospitality with a song each twilight.

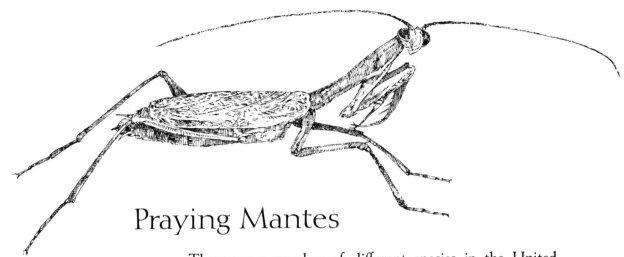

Praying Mantes

There are a number of different species in the United States that belong to the family of mantids (*Mantidae*). The most common one is a species called the Oriental mantis (*Tenodera sinensis*) that was introduced into the United States in the 1890s. Originally released near Philadelphia, the Oriental mantis has multiplied and spread to many parts of the country.

The Oriental mantis is about four inches long when fully grown and has a striking appearance. Its head is small and triangular with prominent eyes. Its long front legs are fitted out with sharp hooks. It has a heavy body and short wide wings. You would hardly think a mantis could fly very well carrying its large body around. But, as mantes are often reported flying into windows on the upper floors of buildings, they obviously can get around.

The praying mantis is one of the few insects that can turn its head from side to side. If you come upon a mantis sitting on the branch of a shrub or a low-growing tree, it will turn its head and stare at you. If you bring your hand close to the mantis, it will raise up and show its powerful, toothed front legs.

When its front legs are folded and its body is bent forward, the mantis seems to be praying. Of course, a mantis really doesn't pray. It's actually in a ready position waiting for an insect or some other small animal to pass by, at which time the front legs of the mantis shoot out and grab. Any small animal caught in that pincer grip is not likely to come out alive. A *praying* mantis really should be called a *preying* mantis.

Once a mantis catches an insect, it begins to feed on it immediately. Its mouth begins to nibble up and down the insect, almost like a person eating an ear of corn. In a short time, everything except the hard outer shell of the insect and its wings (if it had wings) are gone. The mantis is ready for its next victim.

A mantis can feed upon many insects during a day. It will eat bees, moths, flies, ants, spiders, and anything small enough that moves by. The mantis is so quick that it can catch some insects even when they are on the wing.

In nature, mating takes place in late summer or in the fall. The female grows very large with the fertilized eggs in her body. Finding a place on a twig or branch, she begins to give off a frothy material. This is pushed onto the twig. More and more material is added. The eggs are contained within this froth. Shortly after it is given off, the froth hardens and the eggs will be protected through the winter.

The egg case, called an ootheca, is about one inch long and a bit less than one inch wide. At first the egg case is white, but later it turns grayish. In the spring, the young mantes will hatch from the case. The female will not survive over the winter. She dies when the weather turns cold.

A mantis can fly quite well, and you can't usually net it once it takes wing. But if you approach a mantis on a branch, you should be able to get close enough to cover it with an insect net (see page 14). If you don't have a net with you, try capturing it with your hands. The mantis may grab your fingers with its toothed claws, but its bite is not painful, and it won't hurt you. Don't squeeze the mantis too hard or you will injure it.

Drop the mantis into a jar at home and place several twigs in the jar so that the mantis will have something to sit on. Cover the jar with some screening, allowing air to enter but keeping the mantis from escaping. Keep the jar out of direct sunlight, but in a bright spot in your room from which the mantis can look around.

Spray some water in the jar each day. The mantis will drink from a drop on the side of the glass or on a twig. You can even get the mantis to sip from a drop of water on your finger. Hold a drop of water on your fingers just under its head until the mantis bends its head and drinks. After a while, it will learn to drink as soon as you present it with a drop of water.

You can feed your pet mantis with any kind of insect food—ants, flies, grasshoppers, or whatever you can catch. The only drawback is that the food must be moving to attract the mantis's attention. Mealworms, which can be purchased in pet stores, are also a good food. If your mantis doesn't seem to go after an insect, hold the insect in front of the mantis and wiggle it.

Mantes are important animals in nature. By preying

upon insects, they help preserve the vital balance of living things. Some stores even sell mantid oothecas to people who want to keep the insect population of their gardens down without using chemical insecticides.

As a baby mantis grows, it gets too big for its hard, outer skin. It must molt, that is, split its old skin and leave it behind so that a new skin can harden around its body.

During this time it needs water, so wet a piece of paper toweling and keep it in the jar. After about the third molt, mantes are large enough for you to keep them in separate jars. Release any mantids that you cannot care for. A mantis will molt many times until it becomes a large adult.

• A mantis is about the only insect that actually can learn to recognize you. If you handle it each day, it will eventually sit on your finger while you present it with food or water. Watch how it grooms itself. It cleans its feet and face over and over again after it eats, almost like a cat.

Don't try to keep two adult mantes in the same jar. They will equal one well-fed mantis. Not only will a mantis eat another mantis that comes too close, but the female mantis almost always will devour a male mantis after they mate with each other.

If you find a mantis egg case, snip off the twig it is on and bring it home. Keep it in a closed jar somewhere on a shelf. When spring comes, check the egg case each day. One day the mantes will start to hatch. Tiny perfect copies of the adult mantis emerge, trailing down in long strings from the egg case. In a day, you'll have mantes all over the jar. If you keep them in the jar together, they will begin to eat each other. If you can supply them with fruit flies or some other small insects, such as aphids, they will grow rapidly.

moth resting

butterfly resting

Butterflies and Moths

Two of the easiest—and most interesting—kinds of insects to keep in a jar are butterflies and moths. These insects go through four stages in their lives. At each stage they look completely different from any other stage.

Both butterflies and moths belong to the order of insects called *Lepidoptera*, scale-winged insects. More than 7,000 different kinds of moths and butterflies are known in North America. The scales on their wings give them the colors you see. There is no particular way to tell caterpillars of moths and butterflies apart, but the adult insects are usually very different. Butterflies fly during the day; moths usually fly at night. Butterflies at rest fold their wings back; moths keep their wings spread out. A butterfly's antennae are thin and end in a knob. A moth's antennae are feathery and its body is usually thicker than a butterfly's.

A butterfly or moth starts life as an egg. The egg hatches to become a larva. (The larva is the caterpillar stage.) The larva then becomes a pupa. This is a stage in which the insect changes its form completely.

butterfly antennae

moth antennae

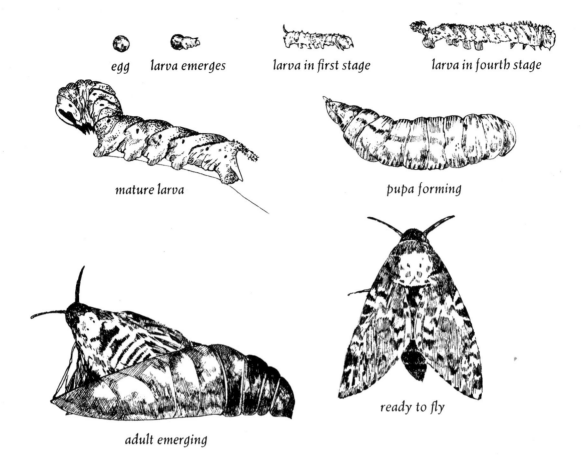

egg   larva emerges   larva in first stage   larva in fourth stage

mature larva

pupa forming

adult emerging

ready to fly

The pupa of a moth is often enclosed in a protective cocoon. A butterfly pupa, called a chrysalis, does not have a cocoon covering. The pupa emerges into its final stage as the beautiful winged insect we call a butterfly or moth.

In the warmer months of the year, the easiest stages to find are the larval stage (caterpillar) and the adult, winged insect. If you find a caterpillar, collect with it the leaves upon which it was feeding. Place the caterpillar in a jar along with the leaves. Sprinkle some water droplets on the leaves each day, and keep the jar covered with screening.

You must furnish leaves as often as they are needed. Since all the caterpillar does is eat, you may have to add leaves to the jar every few days. If you notice that the caterpillar does not eat the leaves you provide, try a different kind of leaf. Once you find a leaf the caterpillar eats, stick to it.

Keep some twigs in the jar for the caterpillar to climb on. When a caterpillar is ready to change to a larva, it will attach itself to a twig. Once the insect turns into a pupa, it is not necessary to add leaves. A pupa does not eat. Keep the jar humid by leaving some wet paper toweling at the bottom. A butterfly or moth will not emerge if the jar is too dry.

Depending upon what kind of caterpillar you collect, it may take little more than a week on up to several months for an adult butterfly or moth to emerge. If you collected the pupal stage in the autumn, the adult will not emerge until the next spring. Pupae should be kept in a cool spot during the winter.

Many butterflies and moths do not eat at all when they become adults. Those that do eat usually sip nectar from the base of flowers. They have long, coiled tongues for this purpose. For these kinds, supply some flowers dipped in sugar water. Experiment to see which kind of insect you have.

If you have several moths in the jar, they may mate and lay eggs. Mating in a jar is more unlikely with butterflies. Butterflies usually need sunshine and flying space to mate. Keep the jar moist when you keep adult butterflies or moths. You can catch adult butterflies in the field with a net or even with a paper bag. Keep them in the cool, moist jar along with some twigs. Adult moths can be collected at night from around an outside light bulb. A female moth caught in this way may lay eggs right in the jar. The female moth has a fatter and larger body that a male moth. Its antennae are also thinner than a male's. If a moth does lay eggs, keep them moist until they hatch. When the eggs hatch, you will have to supply the tiny larvae with leaves of plants that they will eat.

ugh!

•   Many larvae are very picky when it comes to food. You may find that larvae will refuse the kinds of leaves that you supply. Give them other kinds of leaves until you hit upon the right ones. Some larvae will starve to death if you do not supply them with the one or two kinds of plant leaves that they eat. Try breaking a leaf so that the sap is presented to the larvae. Perhaps the odor or some other stimulus will start larvae feeding.

For some species of moths and butterflies you may have to supply a layer of soil for the caterpillars to turn into pupae. The caterpillars dig down into the soil to find a place to pupate. Don't disturb them at this time or they will die. Keep the soil moist but not soggy. After about a week you can gently dig the pupae out and examine them. You can keep pupae over the winter in the damp soil or in a damp paper towel. Keep the pupae in a cool place in the house.

One of the easiest butterflies to find in many parts of the United States is the Monarch. It is reddish brown with black, veined markings. Look around for a stand of milkweed plants when you go on a collecting trip after

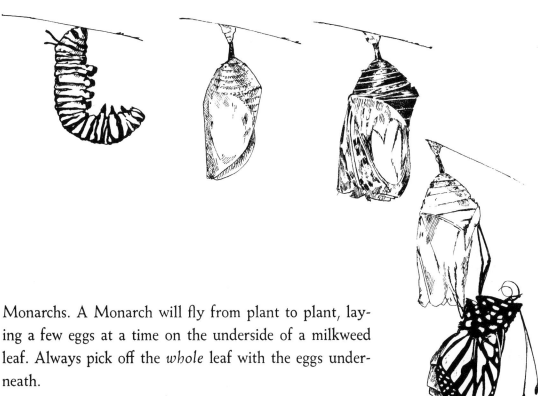

Monarchs. A Monarch will fly from plant to plant, laying a few eggs at a time on the underside of a milkweed leaf. Always pick off the *whole* leaf with the eggs underneath.

At home, place the leaf in a jar. The eggs will hatch in only a few days, and you'll have to feed the larvae with fresh milkweed leaves every day or so. Soon the young larvae will stop feeding and become motionless. Don't touch them. They are molting, that is, going into another larval stage.

After the larvae molt, they will start to feed again, and grow very rapidly. The larvae will molt several more times before they pupate. In about a week or two the pupal skin will split and an adult Monarch butterfly will emerge, open up and dry its wings, and be ready to fly. You should release them if you have more than one or two in your jar.

actual size

Brine Shrimp

Brine shrimp are pets that probably you will not be able to collect. They live in very salty water, such as that at the Great Salt Lake in Utah. But you can buy thousands of brine shrimp in a pet store for under one dollar. That is, you can buy thousands of easily hatched brine shrimp eggs. Pet stores sell the eggs so that they can be hatched and the shrimp used as a food for fish.

Some advertisements in magazines for brine shrimp eggs refer to the shrimp as "sea monkeys." Of course they are not monkeys or even related to them. The scientific name for a brine shrimp is *Artemia salina.*

Brine shrimp are small relatives of the kind of shrimp that we eat. When full grown, an adult brine shrimp is only about 1/4-inch long. Each egg is smaller than a pinhead. One hundred and fifty eggs in a row will stretch about one inch.

150 eggs

In nature, the eggs collect and dry on the shore of their saltwater habitats in huge drifts. They don't hatch unless they are first dried. Dried eggs can be stored and hatched even after several years as long as they are kept dry.

Brine shrimp eggs will hatch in almost any salt solution. You can use ocean water to hatch the shrimp, or you can make your own saltwater. Here's how: Clean out your wide-mouthed glass jar so that no trace of soap remains. This is very important. Fill the jar with water from the tap and let it age for at least a day. That will rid the water of any chlorine left in it. (You can also use pond water instead of tap water.) Mix in six tablespoons of coarse, *noniodized* salt (it will say "iodized" on the box if iodine has been added), a tablespoon of Epsom salts, and one half teaspoon of borax. Stir until all the salts dissolve.

Add a small pinch of brine shrimp eggs, about twenty to fifty. Keep the water in a warm spot in your room, in sunlight if possible. The best hatching temperatures are between 75° and 90° Fahrenheit. The young shrimp, called *nauplius* larva, hatch in about a day, depending upon the water temperature. The warmer the water the sooner the eggs hatch.

If you look at a newly hatched brine shrimp carefully with a magnifying lens, you will see an eye spot and three pairs of antennae. The antennae help the shrimp move through the water when it is just hatched. As it grows, the shrimp will develop many pairs of legs to move it about in the water.

To keep brine shrimp alive you have to feed them. Add a small package of yeast to enough water to make a milky mixture. After all the eggs are hatched, start adding some of the yeast mixture each day to turn the water in the jar just a bit cloudy. The brine shrimp eat the yeast particles and clear the water. If you keep the jar in sunlight, the water will turn green and the brine shrimp will also eat algae.

If you can keep the brine shrimp alive for several weeks, they will mate. The male will clasp the female and they will swim around together for several days. The female lays about two hundred eggs at one time. The eggs float and will stick to the glass sides of the jar. That's why you may find many more eggs in the jar than the ones you added.

The water level in the jar will drop as water evaporates into the air. Draw a mark on the jar with a crayon to show the original water level. From time to time, add freshwater (*not* saltwater) to bring the water up to the original level.

. If you have a microscope or magnifying lens examine some dried eggs before you place them in water. Each egg is shaped like a cup with a rim around it. Now, remove some eggs after they have been in saltwater for a few hours. The eggs have become round, but still show the rim. Perhaps you can observe some eggs when they are just starting to crack open. You still see how the nauplius pulls itself free of the shell but is still wrapped in a thin, transparent covering. The empty shell floats up, attached to

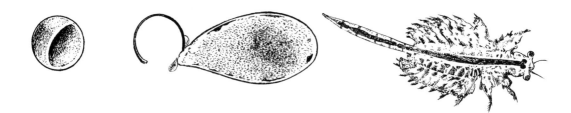

a shrimp that is in a clear sac. After eighteen to twenty-four hours the shrimp breaks clear of the sac and swims away.

Perhaps the most important thing in growing brine shrimp is to make sure they get enough food. You must add some of the yeast mixture to the jar each day. But if you add too much of the yeast, the saltwater will turn bad and the brine shrimp will die. So be careful to add enough yeast to turn the water in the jar *just* slightly cloudy. If you find that you can't find adult shrimp in the jar after a few weeks, don't become discouraged. You'll have plenty of eggs left to start again.

Brine shrimp will hatch in saltwater of almost any strength. Perhaps you would like to make an experiment to see how salty the water has to be to produce the best results. Set up several jars. In one jar place freshwater; in another place slightly salty water. In a third jar place very salty water. Use the same amount of eggs in each jar. And keep the jars under the same conditions of light and temperature. Check the number of eggs that hatch in each jar. You can also perform other experiments to test for conditions the eggs need to hatch, such as temperature, light, and air.

Newly hatched brine shrimp are attracted to light. In a darkened room, place a flashlight at one side of the jar. In a few minutes, most of the shrimp will have gathered in the light. Will they go towards a very bright light as well as a dim light? In nature, the light that attracts brine shrimp is sunlight. Sunlit spots contain more food for the brine shrimp than darker places.

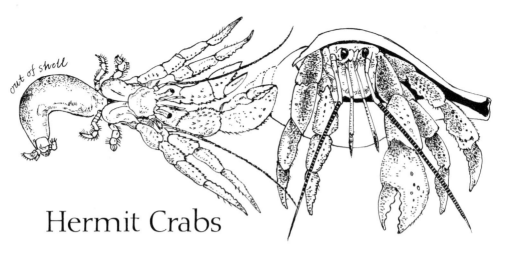

out of shell

Hermit Crabs

Most crabs have bodies protected by a hard shell covering. Not so the hermit crab. It has a soft stomach that provides an inviting meal for many sea animals. To provide a protection for itself, the hermit crab moves into an empty snail shell. The shell provides protection and a home into which the hermit crab retreats when endangered. This shell house is carried around wherever the hermit crab goes.

Hermit crabs are common seashore animals that live on mud flats and beds of seaweed. On some beaches you'll see thousands of them scuttling across the sand. The best time to collect them is at low tide. Don't collect more than one or two for each jar you plan to set up. Also, collect smaller rather than large crabs. Two hermit crabs will fight with each other in your jar. If one is large it may kill the smaller one.

Don't try to pull a hermit crab out of its shell. The crabs have hooks which they use to firmly attach their bodies to the inside of the shell. The head and chest of a hermit are covered by a hard material. The head peeks out when the hermit moves around. The first pair of a hermit's legs are larger than the other legs and have claws at the ends. The claws grab food, fight with other crabs, pinch your fingers, and serve as a protective door when the crab retreats into its shell.

A hermit crab will grow until the shell it lives in is no longer large enough. Then the hermit goes hunting for a new shell house. If many shells are available, it will explore several with its claws. The hermit moves the shell around, turning it over, getting its feel and balance. A hermit crab seems to be a very fussy house hunter. Finally, choosing the shell that is to be its new home, the hermit pushes its body into the new opening and settles in.

You'll need to collect some ocean water for your jars at home. Collect several gallons more than you plan on using. The extra seawater can be stored in jars in a dark place and kept for emergencies. Collect water only from a beach where swimming is allowed because then you can be fairly sure that the water is clean. Make sure there are no nearby sewer outlets or any garbage dumping. You can use large plastic containers with screw tops or plastic bags to collect the seawater. Remember to collect some fine beach sand.

As usual, make sure that the jar is cleaned and rinsed of all soap or detergent. Filter the seawater before you put it in the jar by pouring it, a little at a time, through several layers of strong paper toweling. Rinse the beach sand in running water until it is quite clean. Place a thin layer of the sand at the bottom of the jar. The only other things you might put in your jar are a few smooth beach pebbles.

Now place your hermit crabs in the jar. In a few minutes, they'll stick their heads out of their shells and start exploring their jar. At the slightest disturbance, they withdraw into their shells. If nothing happens, they soon are on the move again, searching for food.

Feed a hermit crab two or three times a week. You can use any animal food, such as a piece of chopped-up earthworm or raw shrimp. Remove any food uneaten after it has been half an hour in the jar.

Keep the jar in a cool place in your house away from direct sunlight. If the temperature goes above 70° Fahrenheit (you can use an aquarium thermometer to check the temperature), wrap a few ice cubes in a plastic bag and float them in the jar. Remove the ice when the temperature drops to below 70°. Remember also to mark the original water level. Use aged fresh water to replace the water that evaporates.

• If the water starts to smell bad or turn cloudy, remove the crabs and keep them moist. Clean out their jar and wash the sand completely with running water. Then replace the sand and add the seawater that you kept in storage.

If you like, you can add a mud snail or two to the aquarium. A problem may arise if the hermit crab decides it wants the snail's shell for a new home. Then the hermit may pull the snail out of its shell, eat it, and use the shell. Snails can use a bit of boiled lettuce or spinach as food.

If you keep hermit crabs for more than several weeks, you will have to supply them with some new shells as they outgrow the old ones. Make sure you wash out any empty

hermit crab investigating a new home

shells you place in the jar. A bit of decaying material in the back of a shell can quickly spoil the water in your jar.

If you have two hermit crabs in the same jar, they may be always fighting with each other. Watch them to see if one always gets the worst of the fight. You may have to remove the weaker crab to a separate jar if you want it to survive. In a larger aquarium, the crabs can find hiding places to escape their quarrelsome neighbors, but in a one-gallon jar there's no place to hide.

A device called a hydrometer will help you to tell the amount of salt in the water. You can purchase a hydrometer at a pet shop. It floats in the water at a certain depth. Markings along the side tell you the reading. Most natural ocean water is about at the 1.025 mark. As water evaporates from a jar, the reading will increase to 1.030 or higher. Adding fresh water brings the reading down again. You can do without a hydrometer by marking the level of water on the outside of the jar at first and adding fresh water from time to time to keep it at that level.

Don't try to keep fish in the jar along with a hermit crab. Most saltwater fish need more space than a one-gallon jar provides. They also need more oxygen than the small amount of water in the jar can hold.

Starfish

Starfish are really not fish at all. They belong to a group of spiny skinned animals (called *Echinoderms*) that also include sea urchins, sea cucumbers, and sand dollars. Starfish might best be called sea stars, but their old name has been used so long that most people will go right on calling them starfish.

Whatever name you decide to use, you will find these sea animals are very interesting to collect and keep. There are many different kinds of stars, and they are plentiful along most seashores. Look for them at low tide. You'll find them under seaweed and in tidal pools left behind by the retreating water. Collect one or two small (two to three inches across) starfish along with a quantity of seawater. Be sure that the water in the container does not get too hot on the way home. Stars are very hardy as long as water conditions don't change suddenly.

Most stars have a five-pointed body, although some species of stars have six, ten, or even more arms. The upper skin of a star is covered with blunt spines. The underside of each arm has many tube feet which can clamp onto an object with great force.

In fact, stars usually feed on clams or oysters by encircling them with their arms and pulling steadily. After a while, the clam gives way to the continuous pressure and opens slightly. The star then turns its stomach inside out and pushes it into the clam shell. The body of the clam is digested right in its own shell.

When many stars invade clam and oyster beds they can destroy thousands. A number of years ago, oyster fishermen used to catch the stars, cut them up with their knives, and throw them back into the sea. Unfortunately, instead of killing the stars, the fishermen were helping increase their numbers. Each cut up star is capable of regeneration, that is, it can regrow its missing parts. So each part that the fishermen threw back in the water became a whole new starfish.

At home, set up a jar for starfish the same way as you would for a hermit crab (see page 83). Be sure to mark the original water level, and refill the jar with aged fresh water when necessary. A star is a meat eater, and will do well on the same kinds of food as a hermit crab eats. Don't use beef or other fatty foods. They will leave an oily slick on the surface of the water. A bit of seafood is best, such as a piece of shrimp or clam. Remove any uneaten bits of food before they foul the water.

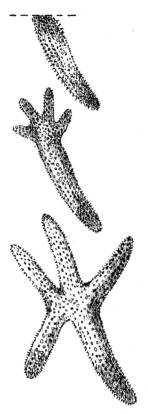

severed arm becomes a new starfish

● Observe how a star moves in the jar. It can walk in any direction. The tip of one arm curves up then pushes out. The animal slides forward as the lead arm pulls together. Use a magnifying lens to observe the tube feet on the bottom of the star. Look at the end of each arm with the lens. The tiny spots of red or purple—called eyespots

—are sensitive to light, but can't really see the way your eyes do.

Try flipping a star over on its back. At first it will lie quietly. Then one or more arms will curve around backward until they touch the sand. The arms on the other side start to curve upward. The star is now almost on edge. In a little while the balance changes and the star flips over on its right side.

Look for an orange spot on the back of the star near a point where two arms come together. This is called a sieve plate. Examine the sieve plate closely. You'll see that it has tiny holes in it, like a strainer. Water enters the star through the sieve plate, then goes into a tube system that extends into each of the arms. The tube feet at the bottom of each arm are moved by the water circulating through the tube system.

Starfish when kept in a jar will not regenerate a lost arm. In fact, the loss of an arm tells you that something is wrong in the jar. Try keeping the jar at a lower temperature and out of the light. If the water begins to smell bad, replace it with some of the seawater you have stored.

Instead of collecting seawater, you might want to use

some of the artificial seasalts now available. *Do this before any collecting.* You can buy a package of seasalts in an aquarium store. They are also advertised for sale in magazines devoted to tropical fish. Be sure you buy a salt that is designed for use in an aquarium. You must stir in the correct amount of salt to aged fresh water. Follow the directions on the package. Wait a few hours and then measure the saltiness, using a hydrometer. The reading should be about 1.025. If the reading is higher than that, add more water; if lower, add more salt. You'll need approximately five to six ounces of salt (about three quarters of a cupful) to a gallon of water.

After you set up the jar with artificial salts it may take several days for the water to lose its cloudiness. Don't dump the stars in the jar when you collect them. Bring the temperature of the water in which you have the starfish to the same point as the temperature of the water in the jar. The best way to do this is to place the star along with some of its water in a small plastic bag. Tie the bag closed with a rubber band. Float the bag in the jar for at least fifteen minutes. This will ensure that the temperatures become similar. Then open the bag and allow some water from the jar to enter. Wait a few more minutes. Continue doing this, a little at a time, until the waters are completely mixed.

If you like, you can try keeping one small hermit crab in the same jar as one small star. Another sea animal that you can try keeping in a jar along with a single star is a sea snail or two. Don't try keeping any more animals than this in a single jar.

When You Let Them Go

Almost surely, there will come a time when you no longer want to keep a particular wild pet in a jar in your home. You may decide that you want to keep a different animal, or that the pet is too difficult to feed, or that you've observed all that interests you for the moment.

But, as you wouldn't push a dog or cat out the door when you no longer want it, you shouldn't release a wild animal pet just anywhere. If you want to get rid of a dog or a cat, you would try to find someone to adopt it. In the case of a wild animal pet, it's not a *person* that you should try to find, but a *place*.

A wild animal pet should be released in the area where you originally caught it, or where others of its kind are already living. Also, it's a good idea to plan on releasing a wild animal during a time of the year when it can survive. Releasing an earthworm in winter is obviously going to result in quick death for the animal.

Certainly as important as the welfare of the wild animal pet is the welfare of the native animals in the area in which you release the pet. Some of the animals in this

book are native to North America. Some are native to many parts of the world. But it would be a mistake to release an animal in a new area where it might flourish and drive out some native species.

From the rabbits that nearly overran Australia when they were introduced to that continent by English settlers, to the starlings that have driven out so many native birds in the United States, history is full of examples of the unpredictable consequences of releasing a species of animal into a new environment.

The animal that you kept so carefully in natural surroundings, in a jar, deserves to be put back in its natural environment when you decide to let it go. Perhaps someone, at some later time, may observe or even collect a descendant of the animal you so carefully replaced in nature.

Books for Reading and Research

Buchsbaum, Ralph, and Lorus Milne, *The Lower Animals*. New York: Doubleday, 1960 (more advanced).

Farb, Peter, *The Story of Butterflies and Other Insects*. Irvington, N.Y.: Harvey House, 1959

Hess, Lilo, *The Praying Mantis: Insect Cannibal*. New York: Charles Scribners and Sons, 1971.

Hogner, Dorothy Childs, *Water Beetles*. New York: Thomas Y. Crowell, 1963.

Hutchins, Ross E., *The Ant Realm*. New York: Dodd, Mead, 1967.

_____,*Scaly Wings: A Book about Moths and their Caterpillars*. New York: Parents', 1971.

McClung, Robert M., *Aquatic Insects and How They Live*. New York: William Morrow and Co., 1965.

Schisgall, Oscar, *That Remarkable Creature, the Snail*. New York: Julian Messner, 1970.

Silverstein, Alvin, and Virginia Silverstein, *Metamorphosis: The Magic Change*. New York: Atheneum, 1971.

Simon, Seymour, *Animals in Field and Laboratory, Science Projects in Animal Behavior*. New York: McGraw-Hill, 1968 (more advanced).

_____, *Discovering What Crickets Do*. New York: McGraw-Hill, 1973.

_____, *Discovering What Earthworms Do*. New York: McGraw-Hill, 1969.

_____, *Discovering What Frogs Do*. New York: McGraw-Hill, 1969.

Smith, Howard G., *Hunting Big Game in the City Parks*. New York: Abingdon Press, 1969.

_____, *Tracking the Unearthly Creature of Marsh and Pond*. New York: Abingdon, 1972.

Stephens, William M., and Peggy Stephens, *Hermit Crab Lives in a Shell*. New York: Holiday House, 1969.

Waters, Barbara, and John Waters, *Salt-Water Aquariums*. New York: Holiday House, 1967.

Zim, Herbert S., *Frogs and Toads*. New York: William Morrow and Co., 1950.

Index